W9-AXA-955

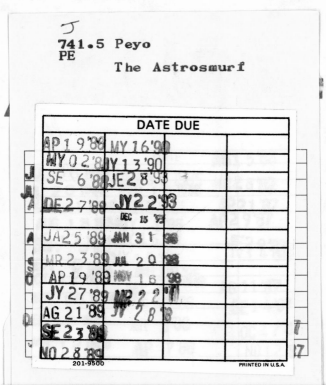

DATE DUE		
AP 1 9 '88	MY 16 '90	
MY 0 2 '88	JY 1 3 '90	
SE 6 '88	JE 2 8 '93	
DE 2 7 '88	JY 2 2 '93	
	DEC 15 '9	
JA 25 '89	JAN 3 1 '9	
MR 2 3 '89	JU 2 0 '9	
AP 19 '89	MY 16 '9	
JY 27 '89	MR 2 2 '9	
AG 21 '89	JY 2 8 '9	
SE 2 3 '89		
NO 2 8 '89		

201-9500   PRINTED IN U.S.A.

Peyo

a SMURF adventure

The Astrosmurf

Written by DELPORTE and PEYO

Translated by Anthea Bell and Derek Hockridge

Random House 🏠 **New York**

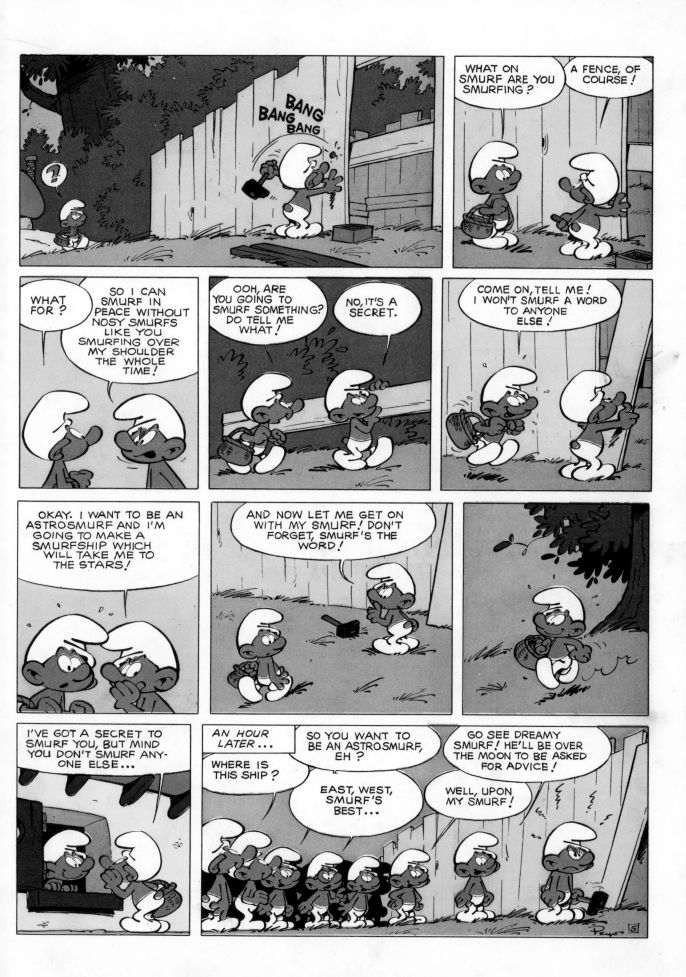

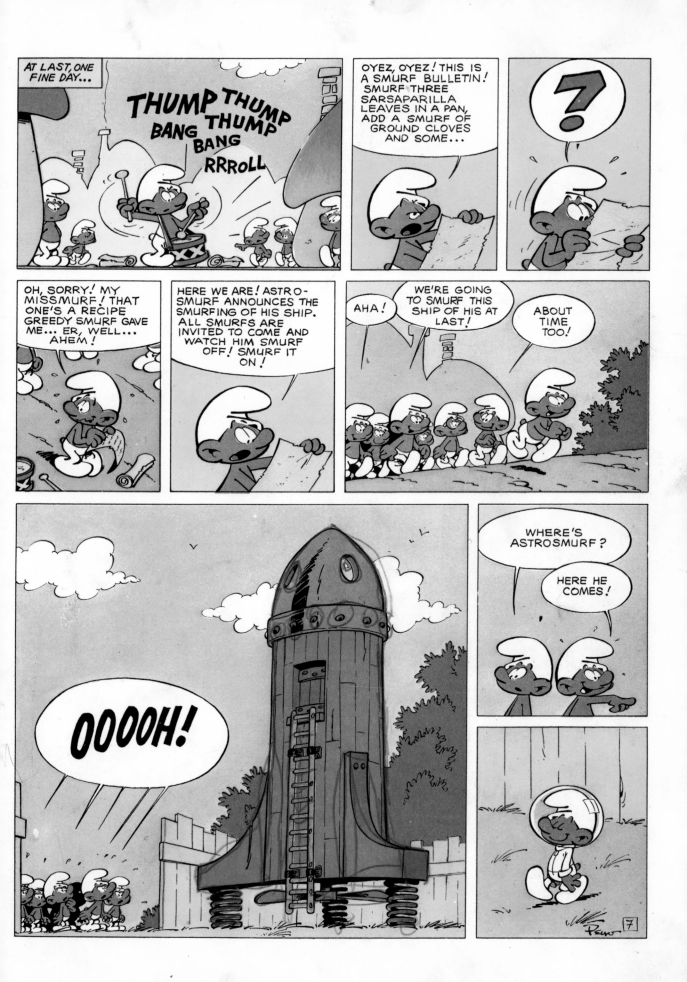

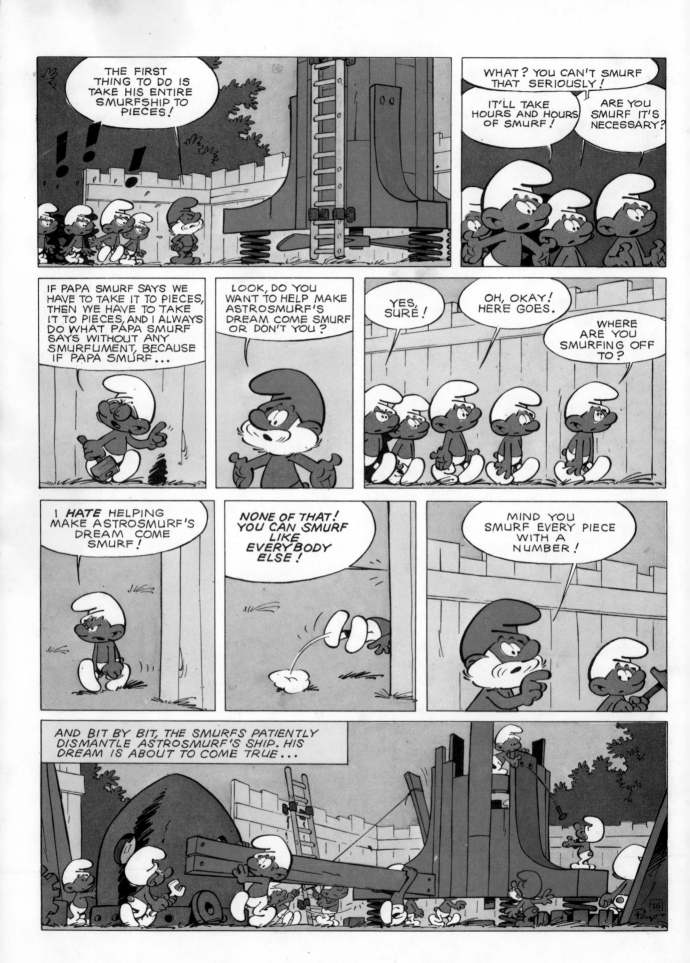

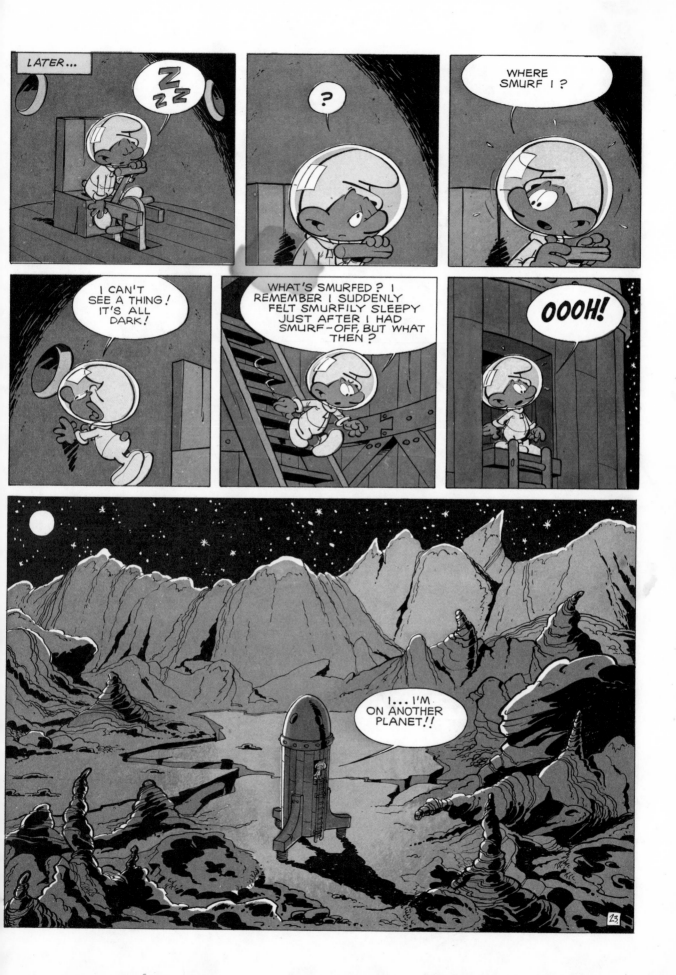

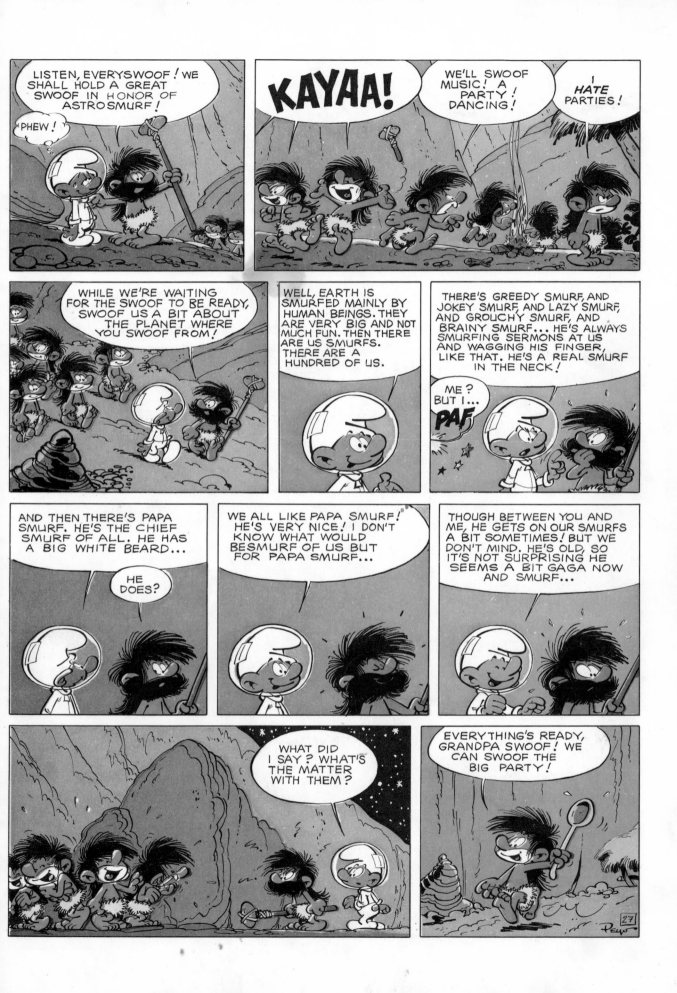

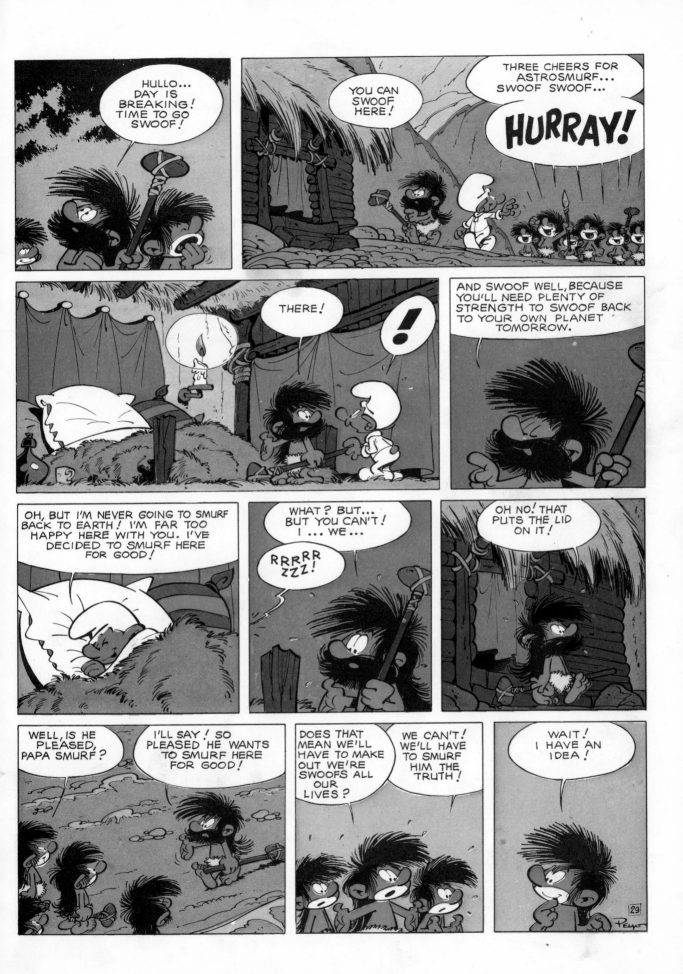

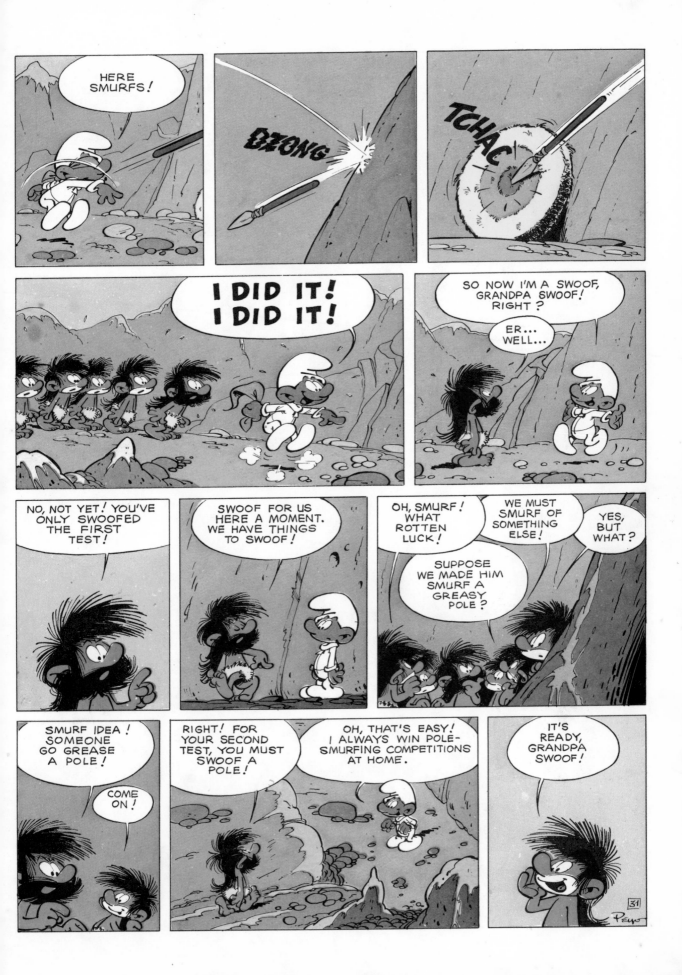

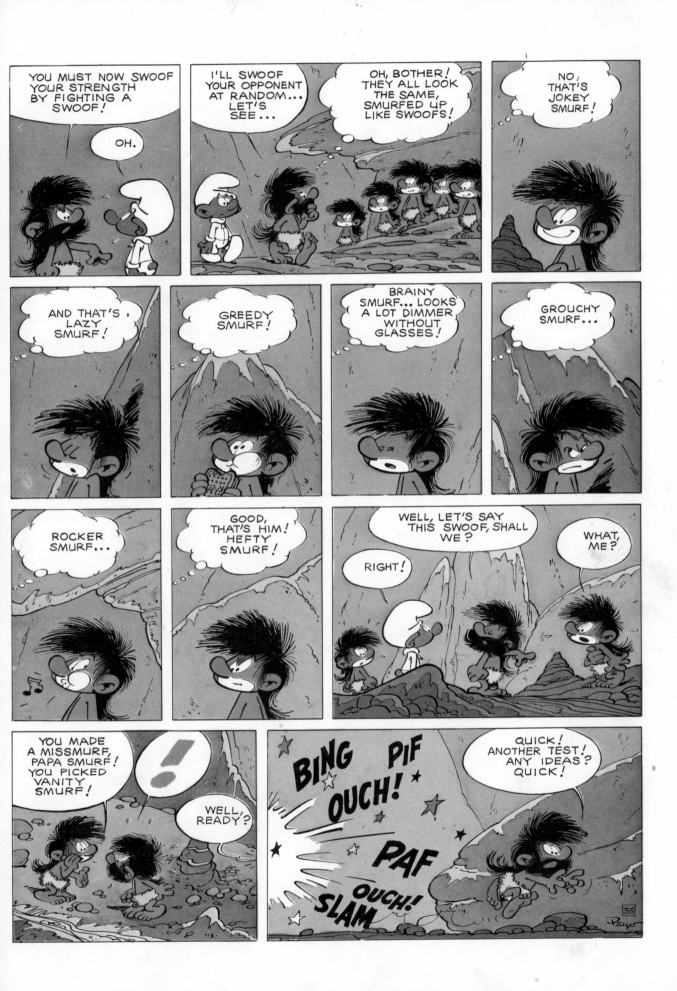

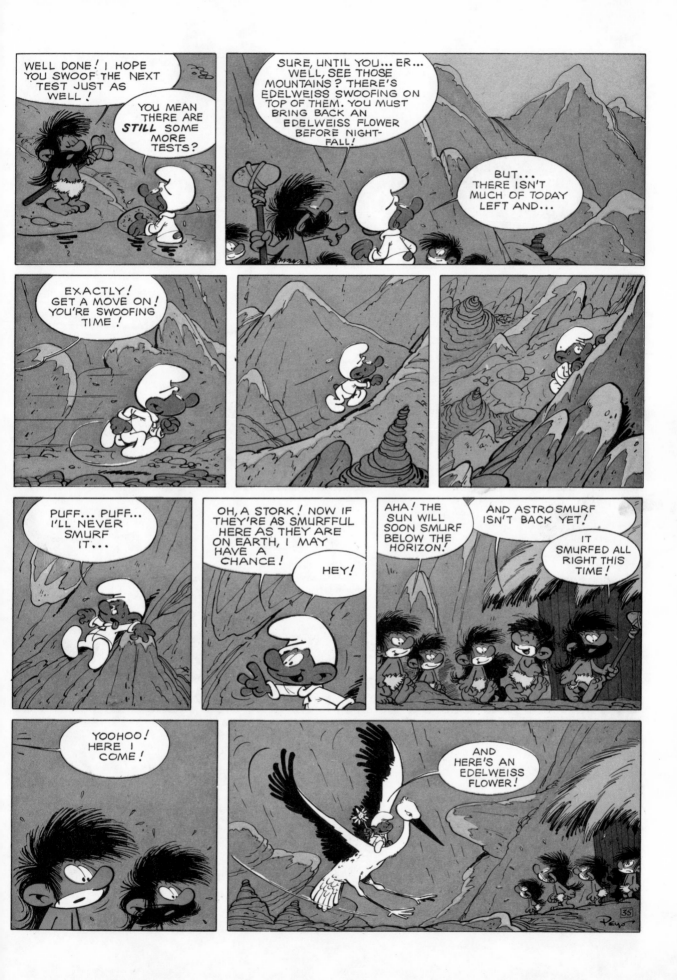

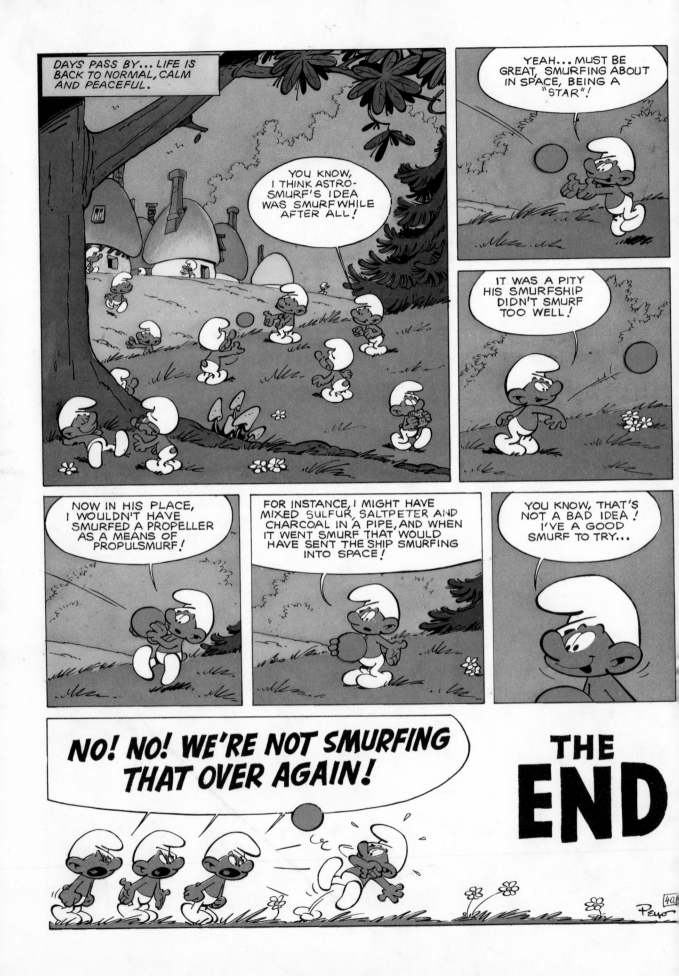